DR. ERNEST DRAKE'S
WORKING WITH D
A COURSE IN DRAGO

EDITED BY

DUGALD A. STEER, B.A. (BRIST), S.A.S.D.

THE SECRET AND ANCIENT SOCIETY OF DRAGONOLOGISTS

This Book Belongs To:

....

....

ILLUSTRATED.

THE TEMPLAR COMPANY:

PUBLISHERS OF RARE & UNUSUAL BOOKS.

*The card certifying your membership of the Secret and Ancient Society of
Dragonologists can be found in the attached envelope. Be sure to sign the Oath opposite
before adding your own photograph to the card and completing your personal details.*

S.A.S.D
Wyvern Way,
London.

October 17th, 1893.

Dear Student,
    I am delighted to inform you
that your application to take
the Secret and Ancient Society
of Dragonologists course WORKING
WITH DRAGONS has been accepted.
    You may now consider yourself
a fully-fledged dragonology
student and, upon signing the
Oath of a Dragonologist, you are
entitled to honorary junior
membership of the Society.
    Yours in
Dragonology,

Ernest Drake

THE OATH OF A DRAGONOLOGIST:

I ....John Joseph Smyth............... do solemnly swear to conserve and protect those dragons that still remain, and in no way to harm them, or reveal their secret hiding places to those who do not believe in them or would wish them anything other than good fortune.

SIGNED ....*[signature]*...

DATED ....25·3·15..............................

This edition produced in 2004 by
TEMPLAR PUBLISHING,
An imprint of The Templar Company plc,
Pippbrook Mill, London Road, Dorking, Surrey, RH4 1JE
Text and design copyright © 2004 by The Templar Company Plc.
Illustration copyright © 2004 by Wayne Anderson,
Douglas Carrel and Helen Ward
Anglo Saxon Runes font by Daniel Steven Smith
Designed by Jonathan Lambert and Nghiem Ta
ALL RIGHTS RESERVED.
3 5 7 9 10 8 6 4 2
ISBN 1-84011-523-8
Manufactured in China

Publisher's note: The publication in 2003 of Dr. Ernest Drake's book *Dragonology, The Complete Book of Dragons* sparked a great deal of interest in the study of dragons, with much subsequent rummaging in antiquarian bookshops and attics in search of new Drake material. This earlier student's volume turned up on the bookshelf of an old public house called *The Canny Lad* in Edinburgh. While we would still prefer not to claim that there was ever a real Dr. Drake, it seems circumstantial evidence for his existence is growing all the time. Nevertheless, this book must be viewed as just another of those 'interesting curiosities' that appear in libraries and bookshops from time to time.

www.dragonology.com

templar publishing

The dangers of seeking homework help even from friendly dragons should never be underestimated.

COURSE PROSPECTUS.

WORKING WITH DRAGONS.
AN INTRODUCTION.

It seems that for many years there has been a requirement for a basic yet thorough coursebook on *Dragonology*. It should provide those students who wish to pursue this subject further with a grounding in its elements that combines useful exercises, information and practical experimentation all in one volume. As a result this book, a companion to my own larger work, *Dragonology—The Complete Book of Dragons*, has been specially prepared for students who would like to begin their basic schooling and are ready, as junior and as yet unfledged members of the Secret and Ancient Society of Dragonologists, to begin their life's work—the conservation and protection of dragons. It is offered in the hope that, in the absence of a properly trained Dragon Master, it will give students a firm grounding.

An ancient saying goes, "When the pupil is ready, the master will appear." The aim of this course is to ensure the pupil is as ready as possible.

Perusal of the *Prospectus* near the beginning of the book will reveal that this course has been divided into a series of twenty-one lessons on dragonology over three levels of achievement, each requiring in the region of an hour to complete.

This book is now issued to all those who feel that joining the S.A.S.D. will enable them to make a contribution to dragon science. Upon successful completion of *Working With Dragons*, further education which will bring you up to the level of Bachelor or Doctor of Dragonology is restricted by interview, or else by the recommendation of a friendly dragon. Any student may tackle the challenges of this course, however, so long as they are prepared to sign the Oath of a Dragonologist. The certificate that is awarded upon completion of the course is found at the back of the book.

I have included along with this work a copy of my own school report, which shows a number of comments and grades that are not at all untypical of a young Dragon Master. It should be noted that the last section of this book MUST ONLY BE ATTEMPTED BY STUDENTS WHO HAVE COMPLETED THE FIRST TWO SECTIONS. I conclude my introduction by wishing you every success, and hope you enjoy— and stay—my course in *Dragonology*.

Ernest Drake

June 1st, 1893

Where on swift wings the dragon flies,
Through distant and uncharted skies,
O'er mountain crags and forests old,
To guard his hoard of hidden gold,
I sought him out, and called his name.
He answered with a jet of flame:
"If you be friend, enter my lair,
If you be foe, then do not dare!"

This series of Elementary Lessons has been created to provide a basic introduction to dragons. It has also been designed so that it gives something in the nature of a test. If the student feels the lessons are too difficult, or does not enjoy them for any reason, then perhaps now is the time for re-evaluation and for deciding whether dragonology ought really to become one's life's work.

Awesome Power and Majesty

ELEMENTARY DRAGONOLOGY.

LESSONS I-VII

Come and Heed My Dragon Call!

LESSON I.
INTRODUCING WESTERN DRAGONS.

The dragon is a large, lizard-like reptile of which there are a number of different species. In order to identify all of the different sorts of dragons that the student may encounter, it is useful to compare them with a standard type. The most obvious candidate for comparison is the common European dragon, *Draco occidentalis magnus*.

2 bat-like wings

Scaly skin

large head

4 clawed talons

Spines on tail

'Arrowhead' tail

EUROPEAN
Draco occ. magnus
LAIR—A mountain or sea cave. SIZE—45 feet long; 13 to 17 feet high. COLORATION—Red, green, black or gold. FORMS OF ATTACK—Flame, tail, claws and horns. FOOD—Cattle, sheep, humans [if no other food available, due to bitter flavour.]

Here are some close-ups of various items of a western dragon's 'equipment'.

Claw

Eye

Wing tip

Horn

Detail of scales

WHEN studying dragons in the field, it is necessary to make notes about the different species, including their habitat and behaviour. The gargouille, *Draco occidentalis minimus*, shares its range with the European dragon. Luckily, the two species are easy to tell apart.

Europe

GARGOUILLE

Draco occidentalis minimus

THE French gargouille is a very common dragon, but it can be hard to spot. It is camouflaged so that it can hide among treetops, or sit unnoticed on the walls of castles and cathedrals. LAIR—Rocky crags, or nowadays, gothic rooftops. SIZE—15 feet long; 8 to 10 feet high. COLORATION—Slate grey or green. FORMS OF ATTACK—Ripping with talons, dropping from height. FOOD—Rats, bats and cats.

Right, common dragon colours.

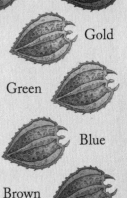

Red   Black

Gold

Green

Blue

Brown

COMPARE the two dragons by filling in the chart below for each species. Use this technique to study dragons in the field.

NO. OF LEGS: 2.4	SCALY TAIL: y/Ⓝ	THIN BODY: Ⓨ/N
NO. OF WINGS: 2	FEATHERY BODY: y/Ⓝ	THICK BODY: y/Ⓝ
NO. OF TOES: 3	SCALY BODY: y/Ⓝ	COLOUR: Green
NO. OF HORNS: 0	MANE: y/Ⓝ	LENGTH: ....
FEATHERY TAIL: y/Ⓝ	FEELERS: Ⓨ/N	HEIGHT: ....

Homework: Find out about the rare Indonesian Komodo dragon, and compare it to the common European dragon using this chart.

LESSON I continued.
IDENTIFYING DIFFERENT DRAGONS.

The student needs to be able to recognise most species of dragon at sight. To assist with this, they should memorise my simple chart [right] before attempting to match the dragons below with their names and descriptions. The first one has been done.

FOUND in low, damp, marshy locations, these creatures cannot actually fly.

Amphithere
Draco americanus

THIS feathered serpent makes its home among the ruined temples of Central and South America.

Lindworm
Draco serpentalis

THIS largely Australasian dragon uses its large back legs to jump after its prey. It cannot fly.

Frost
Draco occidentalis maritimus

DESPITE having only two legs and being unable to fly, this dragon can run at great speed.

Marsupial
Draco marsupialis

THE largest of all dragon species, this creature is native to Africa. It has two legs and two wings.

Asian *Lung*
Draco orientalis

PERHAPS the most well-known of all dragon species, this dragon can be red, green, gold or black.

Gargouille
Draco occidentalis minimus

THIS is the most common variety of Asian dragon, with a large mane and feelers but no wings.

Knucker
Draco troglodytes

SLATE grey or green in colour, this dragon perches on trees or buildings. It looks like a gargoyle.

European
Draco occidentalis magnus

PURE white, or white tinged with blue or pink, this dragon attacks with a fearsome 'frosty blast'.

Wyvern
Draco africanus

Dr. Ernest Drake Says:
"KNOW YOUR DRAGONS."

REMEMBER: a dragon's life—or your own—may depend on your familiarity with this chart showing silhouettes of different species.

WYVERN
[2 legs, wings]

EUROPEAN
[4 legs, wings]

KNUCKER
[4 legs, small wings]

GARGOUILLE
[4 legs, wings]

LINDWORM
[2 legs, no wings]

AMPHITHERE
[no legs, wings]

MARSUPIAL
[2 legs, small wings]

ASIAN *LUNG*
[4 legs, no wings]

FROST
[4 legs, wings]

This poster produced in 1885 for the Secret and Ancient Society of Dragonologists by *Ordo Templis* of Leatherhead & Dorking, Quality Packagers to the Publishing Trade.

Homework: Copy this chart and commit it to memory so that you can instantly recall the details about any dragon.

LESSON I continued.
COMPARING DRAGON SPECIES.

The student will notice that some dragon species look quite similar. There are also sub-species which can be difficult to tell apart, such as the various varieties of Asian *lung*, which are distinguished mostly by the number of toes they possess. Faced with such cases, the student must be sure to note every detail of a dragon they have not seen before in a personal record book, in order to avoid confusion. It may well be that they have found a completely new species. Below, we study the main differences between the frost dragon and the common European dragon.

HOW TO TELL THE DIFFERENCE.
FROST & EUROPEAN DRAGONS:

* FROST dragons can be mistaken for European dragons in both Spring and Autumn, during their annual migration to the Antarctic and back.
* THEY are most active during the night.
* THEY are usually light in colour: white, or white tinged with blue or pink.
* THEY attack with a 'frosty blast'.
* MOST can talk, but prefer to stay silent.

* EUROPEAN dragons are found all through Europe and they do not migrate. They seldom venture any farther than 25 miles from their lair.
* THEY are most active during the day.
* THEY are darker in colour: red, green, black or occasionally gold.
* THEY attack with a jet of flame.
* MOST can talk, and love to do so.

FROST dragons love cold conditions. European dragons only tolerate very low temperatures for short times because fire-breathing requires a certain amount of heat. Wyverns love hot climates. Shade this World map to show the Arctic, temperate and tropical climates each species prefers.

DRAGON chicks can sometimes look different to their parent dragons. It is also important to be able to tell the different sorts of dragon egg apart, and to be able to tell what dragon you are tracking from its footprints. In the exercise below, follow the stylised footprints to see which egg each dragon chick hatched from.

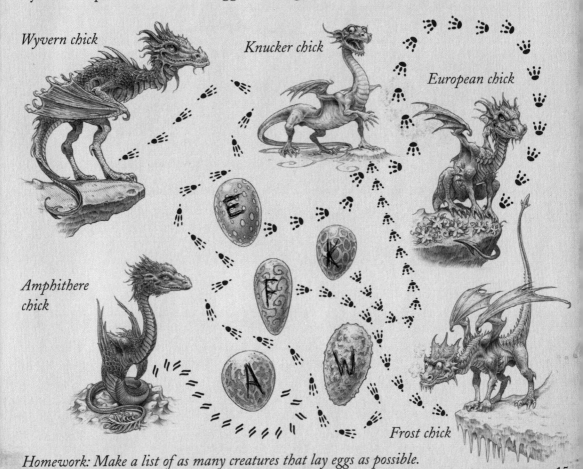

Wyvern chick

Knucker chick

European chick

Amphithere chick

Frost chick

Homework: Make a list of as many creatures that lay eggs as possible.

15

LESSON II.
DRAGON BIOLOGY—FOOD CHAINS.

Each animal or plant occupies a different place in a 'food chain' in the place where they live. The wyvern, for example, lives on the African savanna where there are *producers* of plant food [e.g. grass]; eaters of plant food, called *herbivores* [e.g. zebras]; eaters of animal food, called *predators* [e.g. lions]; and *scavengers* [e.g. hyenas]. In this habitat the wyvern takes its place as *top predator*, feeding on elephants and other large herbivores.

WYVERN *Draco africanus*
LAIR—A rocky crag or circular nest in grass or dunes. SIZE—50 feet long; 18 to 20 feet high. COLORATION—Muddy brown to lime green. FORMS OF ATTACK—Teeth, claws, lashing tail, dropping from great heights. FOOD—Elephants, hippos, rhinos or other large herbivores.

AFRICAN SAVANNA FOOD CHAIN.

TOP PREDATOR..Wyvern
PREDATORS.........................Lion, Cheetah, Leopard, Crocodile
SCAVENGERS..............................Jackal, Hyena, Vulture
HERBIVORES................Elephant, Gazelle, Zebra, Giraffe, Gnu
PRODUCERS..Grass, Trees

IN the Arctic the frost dragon is the top land predator, the sea serpent the top sea predator. Here, food is not produced by plants but by tiny sea organisms called plankton. These are eaten by krill, which are eaten by fish [and some whales], which are eaten by seals and other fish, which are eaten by polar bears, which are eaten by sea serpents and frost dragons.

COMPLETE this chain, putting the Arctic creatures in their correct places:

ARCTIC FOOD CHAIN.

TOP PREDATOR... Sea serpents and Frost dragons.

PREDATORS... Seals, polar bears, other fish.

SCAVENGERS... Fish (maybe Seals etc)

HERBIVORES... Some whales, krill.

PRODUCERS... Plankton

(More are listed below.)

Polar bear, Grey seal, Walrus, Shark, Fish, Krill, Arctic fox, Plankton, Frost dragon.

Homework: In the Antarctic, the frost dragon is involved in a different food chain—there are no polar bears in the Antarctic, but there are plenty of penguins. For your homework research an Antarctic food chain in your local library.

If you're going to get bitten, at least don't get frost-bitten!

MIK MARTIN'S
DRAGON DECOY DUMMY
NOW FUR-LINED & INSULATED
FOR ARCTIC EXPLORATION

—ANSWERS— Top Predator—Frost Dragon; Predators—Polar Bear, Sharks, Grey Seals; Scavenger—Arctic fox, Fish; Herbivores—Krill, Fish; Producer—Plankton.

17

DRAGON BIOLOGY—AGEING DRAGONS.

Dragons grow at a fairly steady rate throughout their lives. Although the upper age limit for each species remains a matter of guesswork, we are lucky that dragonologists have recorded the sizes and ages of some fairly old dragons and, knowing these, we can work out the rough age of a similar dragon, the percentage of its length to that of a dragon whose age is known being roughly the same as the percentage of its age.

Age: 0
Length: 2 feet

Age: ...25......
Length: 4 feet

Age: 100 years
Length: ..16......

Age: 200 years
Length: 32 feet

The illustration above is of my old friend Thorfax, a dragon that had a great grasp of numbers and always knew how old he was. Fill in the missing lengths and ages.

This chart shows the ages of some famous long-lived dragons of the present and past:

Thorfax [European]	304 years
Lung Wei [Chinese]	730 years
Old Hoppy [Marsupial]	95 years
Aveloca [Amphithere]	223 years
Petites-dents [Gargouille]	376 years
Salazaar [Wyvern]	158 years

Here is a list of useful historical questions that can be a handy ready reckoner when trying to age dragons in various parts of the world.

Can you remember the time before there were cows in Australia? (1836, when the first one arrived with some European settlers.)

Can you remember the time before humans learned to fly in balloons? (Before the Montgolfier brothers took to the skies in 1783.)

Can you remember when a herd of elephants crossed the Alps in Europe? (When Hannibal attacked Rome in 218 BC.)

Can you remember before humans started flying a flag made up of stars and stripes in North America? (First flown in 1777, after the American Revolution.)

Can you remember the time before wooden ships with white sails first arrived at the coast of the Americas? (Before Columbus's voyage of 1492.)

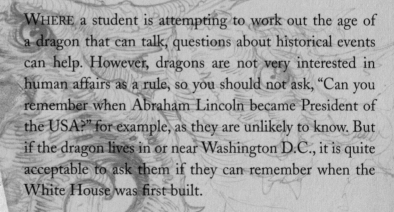

WHERE a student is attempting to work out the age of a dragon that can talk, questions about historical events can help. However, dragons are not very interested in human affairs as a rule, so you should not ask, "Can you remember when Abraham Lincoln became President of the USA?" for example, as they are unlikely to know. But if the dragon lives in or near Washington D.C., it is quite acceptable to ask them if they can remember when the White House was first built.

Homework: Make a list of historical questions based on the area you live in, that you could ask a local dragon in order to estimate its age.

LESSON III.
ELEMENTARY RIDDLE WORK.

As every experienced dragonologist knows, dragons who can talk simply cannot resist a riddle challenge. However, as every inexperienced dragonologist soon finds out, they are usually very familiar with the old riddles and are liable to use them to their own advantage. The solution? In order to become a Master Riddler, you must begin by unravelling some of the classic riddles. See how you get on!

Oft I must strive with wind and wave, battle them both when under the sea.
I feel out the bottom, a foreign land. In lying still I am strong in the strife;
If I fail in that they are stronger than I, And wrenching me loose, soon put me to rout.
They wish to capture what I must keep. I can master them both if my grip holds out,
If the rocks bring succour and lend support, Strength in the struggle. Ask me my name!

The wave, over the wave, a weird thing I saw, Through-wrought, and wonderful ornate: A wonder on the waves, water become bone.

Weight in my belly,
Trees on my back,
Nails in my ribs,
Feet I do lack.

What does man love more than life,
Fear more than death or mortal strife,
What the poor have, the rich require,
And what contented men desire,
What misers spend, and spendthrifts save,
And all men carry to the grave?

The part of the bird
that is not in the sky,
which can swim in the ocean
and always stay dry.
What is it?

What gets wetter the more it dries?

Answers: Oft I must strive.... An anchor • The wave, over a wave.... Ice
Weight in my belly.... A ship • What does man love.... Nothing
The part of a bird.... Its shadow • What gets wetter.... A towel

Homework: Create a modern, up-to-date version of one of these old riddles and test it on your friends. If four out of ten can guess it within ten minutes, you have succeeded. Fewer—your riddle is too difficult, greater—it is too easy.

21

LESSON IV.
READING DRAGON SCRIPT.

When dragons find something useful, they use it for a long time. This explains why they write in runes. The rune alphabet below was engraved on the blade of a Saxon knife or *scramasax* from around AD 800 found in the River Thames.

ANGLO-SAXON RUNES.

F
U/V
Th
O
R
C
G
W
H
N
I
J
Ï
P
X/Z
S

T
B
E
M
L
Ng
Œ
D
A
Æ
Y
EA
Gh
K
Kh

Homework: Practice writing your own name in Anglo-Saxon runes.

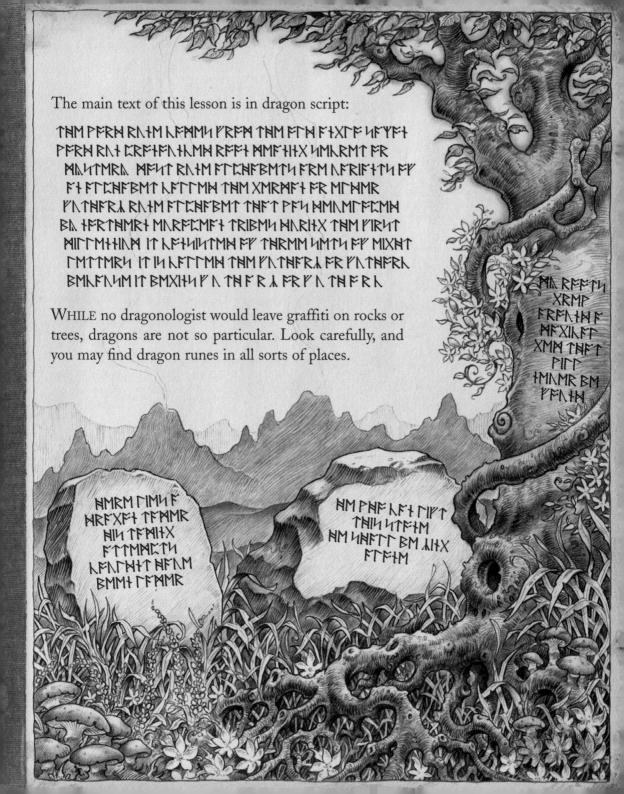

The main text of this lesson is in dragon script:

ᛏᚺᛗ ᛕᚠᚱᚺ ᚱᚪᛏᛗ ᛚᚠᚪᛗᛊ ᛕᚱᚠᚺ ᛏᚺᛗ ᚠᛏᚺ ᚠᛁᚷᚳᚠ ᚺᚠᚠᚳᛊ
ᛕᚠᚱᚺ ᚱᚪᛏ ᚳᚱᚠᛏᚠᛏᚺᛗ ᚱᚪᚪᛏ ᛗᛗᚠᚺᛁᚷ ᛊᛗᚪᚱᛗᛏ ᚠᚱ
ᛗᚪᛊᛏᛗᚱᚪ ᚪᛕᚠᛏ ᚱᚪᛏᛗ ᚠᛏᚳᚠᛒᛗᛏ ᚠᚱᛗ ᚪᚱᚪᛁᚠᛏᛊ ᚠᛁ
ᚠᛏ ᚠᛏᚳᚠᛒᛗᛏ ᛚᚠᛏᛏᛗᛊ ᛏᚺᛗ ᚷᛗᚱᚪᚠᛏ ᚠᚱ ᛗᚳᚺᛗᚱ
ᛕᚪᛏᚺᚱᚪ ᚱᚪᛏᛗ ᚠᛏᚳᚠᛒᛗᛏ ᛏᚺᚠᛏ ᛕᚠᚺ ᛗᛗᚪᛗᚳᚳᛗᚺ
ᛒᚪ ᛏᛗᛏᚺᛗᚱᛏ ᛗᚪᚱᛗᚳᛗᛏ ᛏᚱᛁᛒᛗᛊ ᚺᚪᚱᛁᚷ ᛏᚺᛗ ᛕᛁᚱᛊᛏ
ᛗᛁᛏᛗᛏᚺᚪᛗ ᛁᛏ ᛚᚪᛏᚺᛁᛏᛗᛊ ᚠᛁ ᛏᚺᚱᛗᛗ ᛊᛗᛏᛊ ᚠᛁ ᛗᛁᚷᚺᛏ
ᚳᛗᛏᛏᛗᚱ ᛁᛏ ᛁᛊ ᛚᚠᛏᛏᛗᛊ ᛏᚺᛗ ᛕᚪᛏᚺᚱᚪ ᚠᚱ ᛕᚪᛏᚺᚱᚪ
ᛒᛗᛚᚠᛊᛗᛏ ᛒᛗᚷᛁᛏᛕ ᛚ ᚪ ᛏᚺ ᚠ ᚪ ᚠᚱ ᛕ ᚪ ᛏᚺ ᚠ ᚪ

WHILE no dragonologist would leave graffiti on rocks or trees, dragons are not so particular. Look carefully, and you may find dragon runes in all sorts of places.

LESSON V.
STARTING FIELD WORK.

Field work means, of course, studying live dragons in their natural environments. It is hardly ever necessary to travel far in search of dragons, once you have understood how to read the signs they leave behind them. Here we study some of the more obvious signs that almost any student should easily find nearby.

SIGNS OF DRAGON ACTIVITY

* Quantities of extremely large, smelly dung [depending on the species, can be up to six times the amount produced by an elephant in a whole month].

* Footprints [See lesson III for examples. The gargouille has a liking for 'leaving its mark' by stepping into wet concrete].

* Signs of recent burning [lightning is not nearly so often the cause of wildfires and bushfires as often thought].

* Wisps or tendrils of smoke seen at a distance that, when approached, seem to have no clear origin.

* Bones of dead animals with tooth marks far too large for any 'normal' predator.

* Thick trails of glutinous or slimy matter [in the case of the knucker].

WESTERN dragons do not like to live near humans because we can be very destructive of the natural environments in which they prefer to live. Eastern dragons do not mind living near humans, but would still rather live in a natural environment. However, there is one dragon, the gargouille, which has happily adapted to life in modern cities.

WITH time and a thermometer, you can work out how long ago a dragon was at a certain place by making a dung temperature chart. Never touch the [poisonous] dung, and wash your hands, clothes and thermometer afterwards.

Homework: Find and record all the different signs of dragon activity near you.

Can you identify all the different signs of dragon activity shown in this aerial view of a typical village high up in the mountains?

A. Small, depleted-looking flocks of sheep. **B.** Footprints. **C.** Frightened villagers, with excitable children. **D.** Burned or scorched trees. **E.** Caves full of treasure or the remains of a dragon's meals. **F.** Wisps of smoke. **G.** Dragons flying overhead.

LESSON VI.
THE LEGEND OF THE LAMBTON WORM.

This legend comes from the village of Lambton in England. It seems to be a fairly accurate record of a knucker, of the same type recorded at both the Knucker Hole near Lyminster in Sussex, and of my own local dragon from St. Leonard's Forest.

ONCE upon a time there was a lazy, good-for-nothing young knight, who was the heir of the lord of Lambton Hall. He spent most of his time sleeping, and the rest of it fishing. Of course, in those days fishing was forbidden on a Sunday. But this did not bother the heir of Lambton, and one Sunday he went down to the river, baited a hook, and cast his rod, as usual. He was a good fisherman, but on that day he did not catch anything except for a strange worm-like creature the like of which he had never seen before. Wanting to get rid of that useless catch as soon as possible, the heir of Lambton flung it in a well, and thought that he was well rid of it.

However, in the well the creature grew and grew until it became a large and extremely dangerous dragon. Soon it had crawled out, looking for a new home, and it wasn't long before it found one at nearby Lambton Hill, where some say it grew so large that it could curl around the bottom of the hill three times. From there, it began to terrorise the neighbourhood, and in a short time it had eaten most of the sheep and cattle near Lambton Hill and had set out towards Lambton Hall itself.

The Lord of Lambton didn't know what to do, except to try to please the creature by offering it a vast trough of cow's milk to drink. His son, who had repented of his lazy ways, was away fighting on one of the crusades, and none of the other knights who came to Lambton were able to do anything to defeat the beast.

But just when all seemed lost, the young heir of Lambton returned. He thought that he should kill the dragon he had unleashed, and so he went to ask a wise woman for advice. She suggested that the best thing to do would be to fight the creature wearing a suit of armour covered in very long spikes. But

KNUCKER

Draco trodglodytes

FOUND in damp locations, near food sources such as rabbit warrens. Knuckers have only vestigial wings and cannot fly. LAIR—A deep pond, well or similar 'knucker hole'. SIZE—30 feet long; 3 to 6 feet high. COLORATION—Leathery brown, dull red, greenish blue. FORMS OF ATTACK—A venomous bite, or else constriction. FOOD—Rabbits, deer, farm animals, stray children.

she also said that, if he were really serious about slaying the dragon, the heir of Lambton must make a solemn vow to kill the first living creature he saw after dispatching the dragon, in order that his chances might be even better. However, if he did not perform this deed, then the house of Lambton would be cursed for nine whole generations.

The heir of Lambton thought it would be easy to arrange just which living creature he would see first, and so he was happy to make the vow. He told his father that he would blow his horn upon killing the dragon, so that a hound might be released to run to him. He would then slay the hound and, in this way, he could avoid killing any humans.

The heir of Lambton then proceeded to Lambton Hill and a mighty battle ensued. The

more the monster tried to wrap its coils around him, the more it injured itself, until at last it lay dead. The heir of Lambton sounded his horn but, in his delight that the dragon was dead the Lord of Lambton forgot to release the hound. Instead he ran towards his son, who of course, could not kill his own father, and so, indeed, the lords of Lambton had to suffer misfortune through nine whole generations.

LESSON VII.
EVALUATING DRAGON TREASURE.

As every dragonology student ought to know, Western dragons primarily hoard treasure in order to protect their soft underbellies. Eastern dragons, on the other hand, tend to hoard the treasure they come across excavating their underwater lairs—pearls, jade and such—merely for its unusual and rare beauty. Therefore they are far more likely to be happy to part with it.

DRAGONS are great collectors of treasure but they do not value it in quite the same way as we do. For example, were King Arthur's sword Excalibur to go up for auction it would no doubt fetch many hundreds of pounds. But for the dragon who currently keeps it, it is no more useful than any other tempered steel scratching stick. Were a dragon to get its claws on the famous Star of India diamond, on the other hand, it would no doubt soon be among its most prized possessions. Conversely, the Holy Grail would be considered useless.

BEWARE: Some dragon treasure may have had a protective curse laid upon it, as was the case with the treasure of the aged dragon in the old English poem *Beowulf*.

HERE we will discuss the differences between the way human beings view gems, and the way in which dragons do. Essentially, humans value gems according to their rarity and beauty, dragons for more practical reasons.

Emerald

Diamond

Amethyst

Ruby

Sapphire

Opal

Human Ordering—Gems in Order of Value
i. RUBY [9]   ii. EMERALD [8]
iii. DIAMOND [10]   iv. SAPPHIRE [9]
v. OPAL [6]   vi. AMETHYST [7]
vii. GOLD [3]   viii. SILVER [4]   ix. IRON [5]

DRAGONS do not value gems for rarity, but for hardness—harder gems provide better protection for their underbellies.

Homework: In the chart above, the numbers in brackets represent the relative hardness of each kind of gem. Make a chart that will show the way a dragon would order the gems.

The student who is armed with an elementary grounding in dragonology will find that these lessons broaden and deepen what has been acquired. Now, perhaps, is the time to more actively search out friendly dragons in the field—although the time has not yet arrived when the student should try to deal with any dragon and expect to come away unscathed. Additionally, the student having matured to this level is ready for greater challenges, having no doubt decided that dragonology, if not their entire life's work, may well become a substantial part of it.

I'd be lost without my
COMPASSCULARS
Find your way to a pair near
YOU!

Long ago, and longer yet,
A beast was born none could forget,
And like a loathsome slug or snail,
He left behind a slimy trail,
Which in a maze through forests dim
Led heedless wanderers to him,
And when he'd ask a riddle they
Would answer or become his prey,
Until his reign of terror ended,
By dragonologists befriended.

INTERMEDIATE DRAGONOLOGY.

LESSONS VIII–XV.

LESSON VIII.
INTRODUCING EASTERN DRAGONS.

To learn more about the various dragons inhabiting Tibet and the Himalayas, I set off up Dragon Mountain in the Himalayas in the summer of 1874 to reach the monastery of the Seven Snakes. On the left, you can read the entry I managed to make in my journal, despite suffering from 'altitude sickness'.

DRAGON: Tibetan

DETAILS: Female, red, 40ft, 280 years old

DATE: August 14th, 1874.

LOCATION: Dragon Mountain, near Chogo Ri

TIME: 4 o'clock in the afternoon.

WEATHER CONDITIONS: Clear blue skies!

OBSERVATIONS: I am feeling a little sick and dizzy after my hard climb, with what is called 'altitude sickness'. But never mind! Today I finally met the dragon of Dragon Mountain! Apparently she has lived here for 280 years! I saw her catch a yak for her chick to eat. She killed it with a single bite! The monks say she also eats yetis. Her nest seems to be just a small hollow in the snow, and I can see another egg in it. It has a very curious pattern on the shell.

Perhaps it is the lack of fresh water in their frozen mountain habitats that has caused the Tibetan dragon to evolve so as to lay its eggs in a scrape of fresh snow. The eggshells have very prominent markings.

The Asian lung *lays its eggs in a source of running water.*

Shade Mongolia and Tibet on this map—the main places the Tibetan dragon may be found.

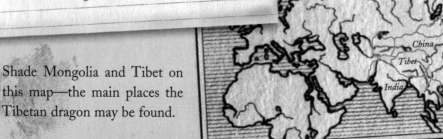

Mongola

China

Tibet

India

TIBETAN DRAGON

Draco montana

BELOW is a painting of a Tibetan dragon. Mark on the picture its *Tail, Spines, Claws, Short Mane* and *Horns*. Tibetan dragons seem to have rather hairy armpits.

WE scientific dragonologists use our field notes to fill in various charts about all of the different species we have seen. Read my journal entry, then try to fill in as much of the chart at the bottom of the page as possible.

a. ....

e. ....

b. ....

c. ....

d. ....

NAME OF DRAGON: ....

LATIN NAME: ....

LAIR OR NEST: ....

SIZE: ....

COLORATION: ....

FORMS OF ATTACK: ....

FOOD: ....

HABITAT: ....

Homework: Above is a Chinese dragon's skull [p34]. Try to sketch a Tibetan dragon's skull.

This picture shows Lung Wei, one of the dragons of Hong Wei Temple, in China. We became very well-acquainted.

ASIAN *LUNG* *Draco orientalis*
LAIR—Usually an underwater cave. SIZE—40 feet long; 12 to 15 feet high. COLORATION—Blue, black, white, red or yellow. FORMS OF ATTACK—Horns, teeth & claws used defensively. FOOD—Mainly fish and birds, particularly roasted swan.

Feathery tail

Long feelers

Staglike horns

Large scales

Mane

Five toes on each claw

Egg, usually carried in foreclaw

洞 *dong* 爬 *pa* 往 *wang*

里 *li* 蛇 *she* 正 *zheng*

THIS dragon gave me a clue to the secret words of the *Hong Wei Invisibility Spell*. He wrote each of the six Chinese characters that make up the spell—but he would not tell me the order in which to speak them.

THE HONG WEI INVISIBILITY SPELL.

LUCKILY, I found the order in which to speak the words in the spell in the *Dragon Sutra of Hong Wei*. Write them out here. Then you will be able to recite the spell.

蛇正往洞里爬

A STUDENT must never underestimate the vital importance of keeping a dragonological journal! Write your own journal entry covering my meeting with the dragon of Hong Wei Temple. Be careful. Should you meet the dragon one day, you may very well need to refer to these notes. Remember: no one knows how long *lung* live for!

Homework: Practise reciting the words of the Invisibility spell until you know them all by heart.

DRAGON: ....

DETAILS: ....

DATE: ....

LOCATION: ....

TIME: ....

WEATHER CONDITIONS: ....
....

OBSERVATIONS: ....
....
....
....
....
....

LESSON IX.
CONSERVING WILD DRAGONS.

It is of vital importance that the student realise that dragons are wild creatures and resist taming. While they can be tamed temporarily by the use of spells or charms, attempts to domesticate them invariably fail. There are thankfully few examples of the kind of enforced captivity exhibited by Phineas Feek and his 'freak fair' [below]. It is important that dragonologists do what they can to help conserve them. Posters can be created to fill this need and help make other people aware of dragons and their plight.

THE above poster, showing tame dragons, unicorns and other supposedly mythical animals being forced to perform at a so-called 'freak fair' was discovered next to the ticket booth at a railway station in Tucumcary, USA in 1879, although no one locally claimed to have any knowledge of the show. The author's attempts to track down Phineas Feek in order to rescue these creatures from his Barnum-like extravagances have proved futile. One can only hope these poor creatures finally managed to free themselves from Feek and that this is the reason he cannot now be located.

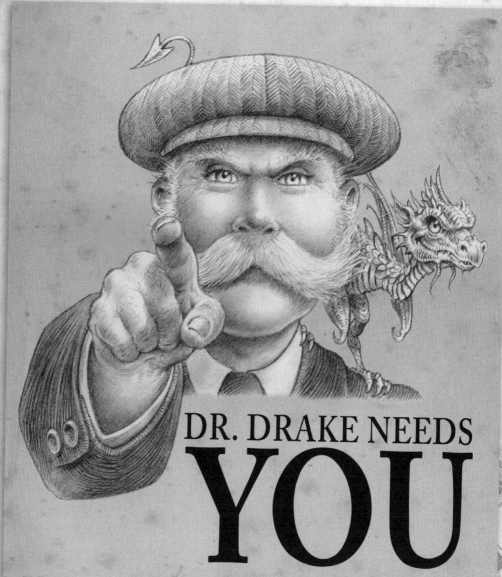

DR. DRAKE NEEDS
YOU

HELP CONSERVE & PROTECT WILD DRAGONS NOW!

Homework: Above you can see exactly the sort of poster the S.A.S.D. believes will help people to understand the need to protect wild dragons. Design your own conservation poster and place it in a prominent location [but remember you may need to ask permission to display it where you would like to].

Note: Frost dragons spend the three darkest months of the Northern Winter [December, January & February] in the Arctic, migrating south to spend the three darkest months of the Southern Winter [June, July & August] in Antarctica before migrating north again. Each migratory journey takes them an average of two months to complete.

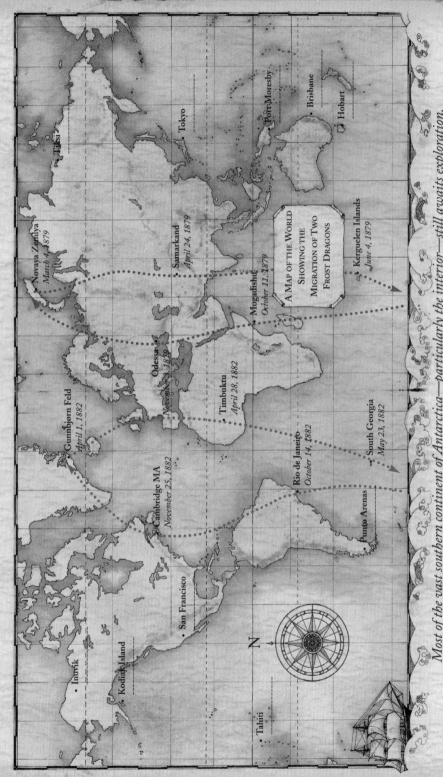

A MAP OF THE WORLD
SHOWING THE
MIGRATION OF TWO
FROST DRAGONS

Tiksi

Novaya Zemlya
March 4, 1879

Tokyo

Port Moresby

Brisbane

Hobart

Samarkand
April 24, 1879

Kerguelen Islands
June 4, 1879

Mogadishu
October 11, 1879

Odessa
November 3, 1879

Gunnbjorn Feld
April 1, 1882

Timbuktu
April 28, 1882

South Georgia
May 23, 1882

Cambridge MA
November 25, 1882

Rio de Janeiro
October 14, 1882

San Francisco

Punta Arenas

Inuvik

Kodiak Island

Tahiti

N

Most of the vast southern continent of Antarctica—particularly the interior—still awaits exploration. Intrepid students are encouraged to join in this great venture if they have the time and resources.

LESSON X.
FROST DRAGON MIGRATION.

Like the Arctic tern, which flies 22,000 miles from the Arctic to the Antarctic and back each year, the Frost dragon is one of the world's great migrators. While their routes over the polar regions are almost completely uncharted—except for sightings by one or two hardy explorers—their migratory paths elsewhere have been tracked thanks to sightings of them [by dragonologists equipped with powerful enough telescopic equipment], flying overhead on clear nights in the Spring and Autumn. On the map I have charted Frost dragon sightings sent in by a number of my colleagues from around the world from 1879 and 1882, but recently some new sightings have come in. Add the dates for these to the map, and draw in the flight path of each beast.

NEW SIGHTINGS OF TWO MIGRATING FROST DRAGONS

I: FIRST SIGHTED IN SIBERIA:
TIKSI, Siberia, March 15, 1883
TOKYO, Japan, April 10, 1883
HOBART, Tasmania, May 15, 1883
BRISBANE, Australia, October 1, 1883
PORT MORESBY, New Guinea,
        October 23, 1883
TOKYO, Japan, November 14, 1883

II: FIRST SIGHTED IN CANADA:
INUVIK, Canada, April 5, 1884
SAN FRANCISCO, USA, April 30, 1884
PUNTO ARENAS, Chile,
        September 15, 1884
TAHITI, Pacific Ocean,
        October 11, 1884
KODIAK ISLAND, USA,
        November 2, 1884

Homework: Unfortunately, the S.A.S.D. map on the opposite page does not include an accurate outline of Antarctica. Find a suitable map of the continent, and plot likely places to search for the dragons sighted there.

An ice-cave typical of the bergs favoured by frost dragons.

LESSON XI.
INTERMEDIATE RIDDLES.

While it is one thing to understand traditional riddles, it is quite another to try to unravel riddles composed by dragons themselves. However, the riddler has a clear advantage in this because dragons tend to make up riddles around a certain number of limited, dragon-friendly themes. My own most prolonged riddle-encounter was with a friendly dragon I know who goes by the name of Lyrax the Lyrical. See if you can unravel some of his riddles for yourself.

Fee Fi Fo Fum,
First I heard my dinner come.
Fo Fum Fee Fi,
Then I smelt it going by.
Fi Fo Fum Fee,
Then I saw it try to flee.
Fum Fee Fi Fo,
Then I touched it with my toe.
Fee Fi Fo Fum,
Now I'll taste it—yum, yum, yum!
I have used five things today
With one name. What is it, pray?
Look above to find a clue
Or my dinner will be—YOU!

Seethed by sizzling searing flames
Seven shiny things I saw,
Hard as shell and round as well
Among treasure on the floor,
Then they cracked and, all unpacked,
Seven baby dragons bore.

Like a coat of shining mail,
On my back down to my tail,
On a snake from tail to throat,
Never on a cow or goat,
Sounds like eight notes on a harp
And you'll find them on a carp.

When a dragon flies,
He seeks it with his eyes.
When a dragon roars,
He holds it in his claws.
When he slumbers, deep,
He dreams of it in sleep,
But there, beneath his head,
It forms his stony bed.

My first's in adventure but isn't in trip,
My second's in river but isn't in ship,
My third is in chalice but isn't in cup,
My fourth's in ascending but isn't in up,
My fifth is in error but isn't in flaw,
My last is in talon but isn't in claw,
My whole is a beast who will eat you for dinner,
Unless in this riddle game you are the winner.

Can you tell what rhymes with moon,
And could be written on a page,
Or on a rock for age on age,
This ancient letter tell me soon!

Where I may rest and you may not,
Upon my hoard of gems and gold,
Where dragon eggs keep nice and hot,
My house, my home, my hall of old.

LESSON XII.

WRITING DRAGON SCRIPT.

While it may be relatively easy to learn to read dragon script—if the person who is using it finds that the script is written in his own tongue—composing in dragon script raises its own problems. However, when it is not possible to talk to a dragon, then it may be that using dragon script will be important. It can be written on many different materials.

The dialogue below shows an example of how to approach a dragon for the first time. It is a record of my first attempts to communicate with Lyrax the Lyrical—and in order to approach him I wrote my messages on strips of bark and threw them into his cave. As I found was usual for him, Lyrax answered me in rhyme, scratching out his replies on the backs of the pieces of bark. He did not reply to my first message.

Dr. D:	ᚺᛖᛚᛚᚩ
Lyrax:	....
Dr. D:	ᚳᚩᛗᛖ ᚠᚩᚱᛏᚺ ᛦᚩᚢ ᛋᚳᚨᛚᛦ ᛒᛖᚨᛋᛏ
Lyrax: :	ᚨᚾᛞ ᛦᚩᚢ ᛋᚺᚨᛚᛚ ᛒᛖ ᛗᛦ ᚠᛖᚨᛋᛏ
Dr. D:	ᚾᚩᛏ ᛏᚺᚩᚢᚷᚺ ᛦᚩᚢ ᚠᛖᛖᛚ ᛋᛏᚱᚩᚾᚷ ᚾᛖᛖᛞ
Lyrax: :	ᛁ ᚠᛖᛖᛚ ᚨ ᚾᛖᛖᛞ ᛏᚩ ᚠᛖᛖᛞ
Dr. D:	ᛁᛚᛚ ᚳᚩᛗᛖ ᛁᚾᛏᚩ ᛦᚩᚢᚱ ᚳᚨᚢᛖ
Lyrax:	ᛞᚩ ᚨᚾᛞ ᛦᚩᚢᚱ ᛞᚨᚾᚷᛖᚱᛋ ᚷᚱᚨᚢᛖ
Dr. D:	ᚨᚾ ᚨᛗᚢᛚᛖᛏ ᛁ ᛋᛖᛖᛣ
Lyrax:	ᛦᚩᚢ ᛗᚢᛋᛏ ᚾᚩᛏ ᛖᚢᛖᚾ ᛈᛖᛖᛣ
Dr. D:	ᛦᚩᚢᚱ ᛏᚱᛖᚨᛋᚢᚱᛖ ᛗᛁᚾᛖ ᛋᚺᚨᛚᛚ ᛒᛖ
Lyrax:	ᛏᚺᚨᛏ ᛞᚨᛦ ᛦᚩᚢᛚᛚ ᚾᛖᚢᛖᚱ ᛋᛖᛖ
Dr. D:	ᛁᛚᛚ ᚱᛁᛞᛞᛚᛖ ᛦᚩᚢ ᚨ ᚱᚺᛦᛗᛖ
Lyrax:	ᛁᛏ ᚹᛁᛚᛚ ᛒᛖ ᛦᚩᚢᚱ ᛚᚨᛋᛏ ᛏᛁᛗᛖ

Homework: Write out your own dialogue with Lyrax the Lyrical on the right.

LYRAX: ᚹᚼᚠ ᛁᚼᛁᛏ ᚷᚨᛗᛁ ᛏᚼᛖᚱᛖ ᚠᚨᛏᚼᛁᚼᛗ ᚠᚢ ᚺᛁ ᛚᚨᛁᚱ

YOU:

LYRAX: ᛁᛚᛏ ᛚᚠᚨᛗ ᚠᛏᚼ ᛗᛖᛖᛏ ᚨᚠᚨ ᚠᛏᚼ ᛏᚼᛖᛏ ᛖᚨᛏ ᚨᚠᚨ

YOU:

LYRAX: ᛁᚠ ᚨᚠᚨ ᛚᛏᚠᚹ ᚼᚱ ᚼᚱᚠᚨᛗ ᚨᚠᚨ ᛚᚠᛏᚼᛏ ᛒᛖ ᚠ ᚠᚠᚨᛗ

YOU:

LYRAX: ᚨᚠᚨ ᛗᛖᛖᛗ ᛚᛗᚱᚨ ᚨᚠᚨᚷ ᛏᚠ ᚷᚠ ᚼᚱᚠᚷᚨᛏ ᚠᛖᚨᚷ

YOU:

LYRAX: ᛚᚠᚱᚼᛏ ᚼᛁ ᛚᚠᚨᚷᚼᛏᛖᚱ ᚹᚼᛏ ᚠᚱᛖ ᚨᚠᚨ ᚠᚠᛏᛖᚱ

YOU:

LYRAX: ᚷᚠᚨᚼᛒᛖᛗ ᚷᚠᚨᚼ ᛚᛏᛚᛚ ᚨᚠᚨ ᚼᚠᛗ ᛚᚠᛏᚼ ᚠᚠ ᛚᛏᛚᛚ

LESSON XIII.
BEGINNING DRAGON MAGIC.

Magic and charms are always a difficult part of dragonology—in fact, most scientific dragonologists find most magic dubious and downright dangerous. However, as it forms such an essential part of dragon legend [as opposed to science] I have included a few notes on how to make a simple talisman. Talismans, amulets and charms [see Glossary] have been used for millennia, either for defensive purposes, or aggressive ones, or sometimes—sanctioned by the dragons themselves—as powerful dragon attractors.

Above, the ancient, fabled and powerful TALISMAN OF MASTER MERLIN, described by the monk Gildas Magnus in *Ars Draconis*, 1465.

Right, SPLATTERFAX, war-amulet of the Viking Rus. Designed to call down a hail of rocks on its unfortunate victims, it is no surprise that dragons confiscated it long ages past. Said to be made from skystone—iron that fell to Earth as part of a meteorite.

Note: While amulets and charms do not require spells to work, talismans often require the recitation of the correct 'magic words'.

Right, a so-called "LUCKY DRAGON" CHARM—only sold to the unsuspecting and gullible. Believe me, you'll be much luckier if you never set eyes on one.

ABRAMELIN'S DRAGON ATTRACTOR.

NEEDFUL THINGS: A sheet of iron in the shape of an octagon [eight-sided figure] six inches across; a large diamond cut into the shape of a teardrop; gold for plating.

PROCEDURE: Plate the sheet of iron with the gold. Cut a hole in the centre and fix the diamond, using an iron clasp, to a rod that drops through the centre hole. The diamond should freely rotate. Use an engraving tool to mark out the images of the eight chief dragon types [see illustration]. Engrave the Attractor Spell below in runes around the outside of the gem.

TO USE, go to an area where there are likely to be [friendly] dragons. Set the diamond pointer so it is turned towards the dragon you wish to attract, and call out the spell:

DRACO-RACO-ACODRAC!

[Note: Scientific dragonologists believe it is really the gem that causes dragons to be attracted, but you might as well say the words too.]

Homework: Make a practise version of Abramelin's Dragon Attractor by covering card with foil [tin will suffice]. Using your ingenuity, fix a piece of shiny card cut like a diamond in the centre, so it can rotate. Lacking the precious gem it will not have much power, but you never know!

LESSON XIV.
IN THE LABORATORY.

Although a fully-functional dragonological laboratory will be beyond the means of most dragonology students, there are certain scientific experiments that can be performed without the need for a great deal of expensive equipment.

PURPOSE: To evaluate the corrosive properties of knucker venom.

MATERIALS: A quantity of fresh knucker venom [donated, if possible]. A crystal vial & crystal mixing bowl [for some reason crystal is not corroded by knucker venom]. Materials to be tested—crystal, diamond, granite, wood, clay, marble, meat, bone. An accurate chronograph or watch.

PROCEDURE: Place 1 oz. of the material to be tested in the crystal mixing bowl. Pour around 1/4 gill of the venom on the material noting the time taken, if any, for the substance to dissolve and noting any other effects. Stand well back when the experiment is in progress. Between testing the different substances, make sure that the crystal bowl is completely clean. This will require repeated washing in water, as the first washings will result in the production of a large amount of steam. Alligator skin gloves should be worn when scrubbing away residue.

It will take the diligent student some years to put together a really complete modern laboratory.

Always remember to label your scientific specimens as clearly as possible.

EXPERIMENT RESULTS.

MATERIAL	TIME TO DISSOLVE	OBSERVATIONS
Diamond	did not dissolve	no reaction
Crystal	did not dissolve	no reaction
Granite	between 5 and 10 minutes	gave off almost a grey 'flame'
Marble	3 minutes	an intermittent stream of blue smoke
Clay	10-15 seconds	a slow stream of grey smoke
Wood	1-2 seconds	a very large cloud of grey smoke
Hair	1-2 seconds	a dense cloud of thick, black smoke
Meat	immediate	a sudden flash of light, smoke

The inquiring mind will have no problems devising their own experiments.

The essence of a modern scientific experiment is that it can be replicated exactly to test its findings again.

Try the following experiment to determine the relative hardness of different sorts of materials: diamond [optional, do not borrow your mother's jewellery without permission], dragon claw [if you cannot source a dragon's claw, use the hardest object you can find], stone, paper, bark, card, chalk.

First, write up the purpose, materials [see above] and procedure. Secondly perform the experiment—which in this case involves using each item to try and scratch each of the other items, noting which they will scratch, and which they will not. Finally, tabulate the results, noting the materials in levels of relative hardness. If you have access to a diamond, the dragon claw should come second.

Homework: The smell of dragon dung is known to scare away almost all predators, large and small. Devise an experiment to test the effective range of different quantities and types of dragon dung. Do not ever handle dung yourself. Only use DRAGON dung for the experiment.

LESSON XV.
A LEGEND OF THE DRAGON KINGS.

On my expedition to China to seek out the ancient and hidden temple of Hong Wei, high in the mountains, my companion Miss Ta told me a number of dragon legends to pass the time. It seems that in China, as in many areas of the world, dragons have been so good at avoiding unnecessary contact with humans, that they have luckily managed to retain the status of purely mythical creatures. One of Miss Ta's legends concerns the founding of the four great rivers of China—the Heilongjian, in the far north; the Huanghe, or Yellow River, in the centre; the Changjiang, or Yangstze, in the south; and the Zhujiang, or Pearl River, in the far south.

Long ago, there were no rivers or lakes in China. Rain fell from time to time to water the people's crops, but the only large body of water in the world was the Eastern Sea. At the time this body of water was home to the four Chinese dragon kings—the Black Dragon, the Long Dragon, the Pearl Dragon and the Yellow Dragon [who later gifted Emperor Fu Hsi with the vital secret of writing]. All of these dragons, like everything else on earth, were under the rule of the Jade Emperor, who is also known as Father Heaven, or the August Personage of Jade. He lived with his court in his heavenly palace that lies far above the clouds and from there oversaw the affairs of the world.

Now one day, the four dragon kings had risen out of the sea to fly around in the sky when the Pearl Dragon suddenly noticed that everything was not as it should be on Earth. All the people had grown very thin, for there had been no rain for a long time, and their crops were withering and turning yellow in the fields. The Pearl Dragon saw them putting out fruit, cakes and other offerings, as they prayed to the Jade Emperor.

"Oh great Jade Emperor," called out one particularly thin woman who was carrying a little boy on her back, "please send us some rain so that we may grow rice for our children to eat!"

When the Pearl Dragon pointed this out to the other dragon kings, they all became greatly concerned.

"These poor people are sure to die if there is no rain soon!" exclaimed the Yellow Dragon.

"We must ask the Jade Emperor for help at once!" suggested the Long Dragon.

And so all four dragons sped away up into the clouds to visit the Jade Emperor in his heavenly palace.

In the palace the Jade Emperor was not pleased to see the four dragon kings—he was enjoying listening to some especially delightful fairy music.

The Long Dragon stepped forward and said, "Your Majesty, I beg you to send some rain to the people quickly, for their crops are withering and dying in the fields."

But the Jade Emperor wanted to continue listening to the lovely music, and so he pretended to agree to the Long Dragon's request.

"Yes, all right," he said. "You four go back down to Earth and I will send some rain tomorrow."

The four dragon kings were happy with this answer, and so they returned to earth. But nearly two weeks passed by, and not a single drop of rain had fallen. By now the people were getting so hungry that they were

trying to eat grass and roots in order to feed themselves.

The four dragon kings felt very sorry, because they now realised that, this time, the Jade Emperor had not paid any attention to the problems in China. It was up to them to help solve the problem. So they all wondered what to do and eventually the Long Dragon had an idea as he gazed at the Eastern Sea.

"There is so much water in this sea where we live," he said. "Why don't we use that to help the people? We can scoop it up and spray it towards the sky. Then it will be just like rain drops!"

The three other dragons agreed that this seemed like a good plan, but they were all worried, because they knew that the Jade Emperor would be angry if he discovered that they had helped the people without asking his permission.

"Well, I am happy to risk the anger of the Jade Emperor," exclaimed the Yellow Dragon.

"Indeed," agreed the Black and Pearl Dragons. "We must do anything necessary in order to help the people."

So the four dragon kings flew back and forth, scooping up the water from the sea in their mouths and, with a noise like thunder, carrying it far over the land where they sprayed it all over the earth. The people below were happy that it was raining at last, and they came out and danced for joy.

Soon the rice and wheat and sorghum in the fields started to look a lot healthier.

But the god of the sea had been watching what the four dragon kings had been doing, and he reported what he had seen to the Jade Emperor.

The Jade Emperor was outraged that the four dragons had acted without his permission, and he soon called out his heavenly generals and their troops to arrest them. Soon the four dragon kings were brought to the Jade Emperor's heavenly palace.

"Fetch me four mountains!" the Jade Emperor told the Mountain God. "These four dragons must never escape to disobey me again!"

And so it was that the Mountain God summoned up four great mountains, and pressed them down on the four dragons, one in each part of China.

But the story does not end there, for the four dragons were all determined to do what they could to make sure that the people never ever went without water again. They transformed themselves into the first rivers in China, flowing out of four mountains. The Black Dragon became the Heilongjian in the far north, the Yellow Dragon became the Huanghe, or the Yellow River, in the centre, the Long Dragon became the Changjiang, or Yangstze, in the south, while the Pearl Dragon became the Zhujiang, or Pearl River, in the far south. And those four rivers are still flowing to this very day.

Having reached this level of achievement, the advanced student of dragonology can be left much more to their own devices. They are assumed to be capable of creating their own programme of work, suitable to the area in which they live, and of going out into the field to study actual dragons. While tips and hints are provided, it is now up to the student themselves to contribute to our growing knowledge of dragons and, where they feel it is suitable, pass on that knowledge to others. Wide reading about dragons is essential. Additionally, important works of Natural History should now be consulted, as well as any work of fiction that includes dragons: it is a little-known fact that most authors who write about dragons are Dragon Masters in their own right.

ADVANCED DRAGONOLOGY.

LESSONS XVI-XXI

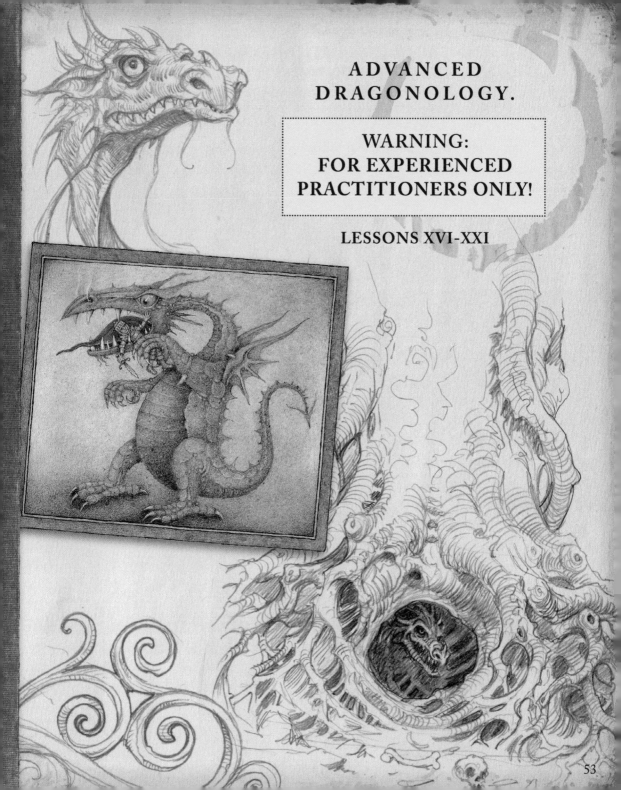

LESSON XVI.
INTRODUCING OTHER DRAGONS.

Once [incorrectly] thought to be extinct, marsupial dragons are a little known species, worthy of more diligent study. Once widespread throughout all of Australia, the marsupial dragon's range has now become restricted to the Blue Mountains in the south east.

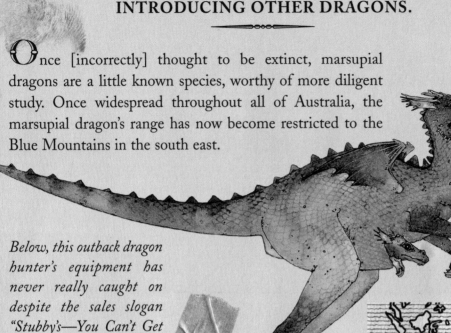

Below, this outback dragon hunter's equipment has never really caught on despite the sales slogan "Stubby's—You Can't Get Enough!"

BEV STUBBY'S
BACK O' BOURKE BUSH HAT

PRICE ON APPLICATION

GOING AFTER MARSUPIAL?
DON'T LET "OLD HOPPY"
GIVE YOU THE RUNAROUND!

Diamonds are a dragon's best mate
(and they keep the flies away, too).

MARSUPIAL *Draco Marsupialis*
LAIR—Rocky caves in Blue Mountain eucalypt forests. SIZE—25 feet long; 15 to 18 feet high. COLORATION—Green or blue-ish. FORMS OF ATTACK—Flaming breath, lashing tail, kicking feet, boxing 'fists'. FOOD—Any large marsupials, sometimes smaller prey.

Homework: Speak to people who know your local area, to research if there might be any places nearby like 'Hoppy's Hole', or suitable caves, old wells or 'knucker holes'.

*Hoppy's Hole,
Australia*

IT may be that the Valley of the Winds in Kata Tjuta [the Olgas], a large rock formation near Uluru [Ayers Rock] in the centre of Australia, is a traditional 'dragon trap'. However, Hoppy's Hole, a secret location near King's Canyon, is certainly one, for here, natural features of the landscape provide a narrowing gorge, down which humans have lured marsupial dragons for centuries in order to capture them. Sadly, it seems that marsupial dragons, like some other marsupial creatures of Australia, are gradually becoming extinct due to the success of one very successful creature—Man!

Some people believe that the great continents of Africa, the Americas and Australia were once connected, aeons ago. While there is yet no proof of this, it may explain why there are marsupials in both South America and Australia.

55

One of the greatest dangers in studying little-known beasts such as dragons is believing everything one reads about them. While this can provide amusement for the amateur—and even intermediate—dragonologist, at the advanced level one must be able to discern with accuracy what is likely to be true from what is bound to be false.

The cockatrice and basilisk are often confused. However, the cockatrice is not a dragon as such, but is another descendent of the flighted archaeopteryx, and so also a relative of the semi-mythical phoenix.

COCKATRICE
Gallicus halitosis

LAIR—Mediterannean mountain forests, usually among pines. SIZE—3 feet long; 1 to 2 feet high. COLORATION—Red or maybe green. FORMS OF ATTACK—Poison droplets in breath. FOOD—Whatever it chances across, except for toads or snakes, which it will not eat.

2 years, 3 months to go...

If looks could kill... The cockatrice, like the basilisk, is said to kill with a glance. This is, of course, nonsense.

The cockatrice kills its victims by breathing on them.

LEGEND says the birth of a cockatrice occurs when a hen's egg is hatched by a snake or by a toad. In reality, toads and snakes only help to hatch genuine cockatrice eggs, and are among the few creatures this animal will not attack.

BASILISK FACTS AND MYTHS.

MYTH: Basilisks are mythical creatures that have never existed.
FACT: Basilisks are shape-shifters and so are very hard to spot.
MYTH: Basilisks can kill with a single glance.
FACT: There is no antidote to their venomous bite.
MYTH: Basilisks look like snakes with a cockerel's head.
FACT: No one knows what their 'real' shape is like.
MYTH: Myths of basilisks started with Pliny's description of a cobra.
FACT: Hanging a basilisk corpse from the rafters helps deter spiders and swallows from coming into your house.

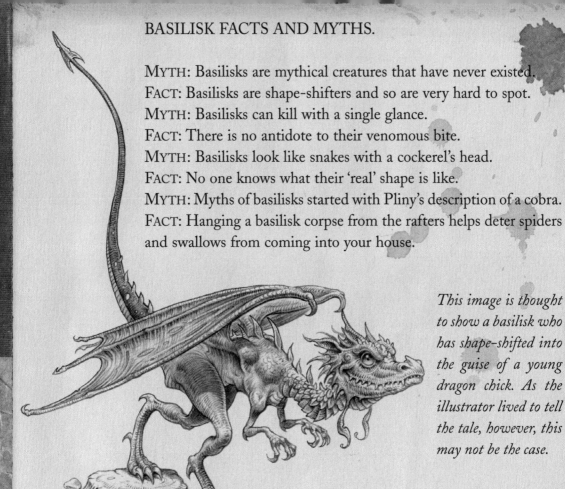

This image is thought to show a basilisk who has shape-shifted into the guise of a young dragon chick. As the illustrator lived to tell the tale, however, this may not be the case.

THOSE who study wild dragons take mirrors with them when they go searching for basilisks. This is because, faced with two enemies—the student, and their own reflection, the basilisk will judge themselves the more dangerous and attack the mirror, leaving the student free to make notes.

BASILISK *Draco basiliskos*
LAIR—Among the bluebell woods of chalk downland. SIZE—4 feet long; 2 to 3 feet high. COLORATION—Brown or green. FORMS OF ATTACK—Extremely venomous bite. FOOD—Whatever it comes across, but it prefers tender meat—the younger the better.

Homework: Write out a list of true [but surprising] and false [but widely believed] facts about another animal.

ALL-AMERICAN DRAGONS.

The Americas are the home of some of the world's most interesting dragons, which have been extensively studied by the American Dragonological Society.

AMPHITHERE
Draco americanus mex

Some of this dragon's feathers are up to 4 feet long. Made into quills, they would take at least two people to manhandle.

The tail feathers of the Amphithere are the most ticklish of them all.

The wingspan of these awesome creatures reaches nearly 30 feet. They also have enormous tongues— up to 6 feet in length.

When attacking small prey [such as humans], the Amphithere only bothers to use the tip of its tail to strangle its victim.

MEXICAN legends tell of the god Quetzalcoatl, who is sometimes shown as a man and at other times as a feathered serpent. Images of him often adorn the huge pyramid structures of the Aztecs. However, no record of the Amphithere appears in the 'Archives of the Indies', the documents relating to the conquest and colonisation of the Americas by the Spanish conquistadores. It seems likely that knowledge of them was suppressed in order to encourage immigration!

Amphitheres are highly solitary creatures. However, each year they gather in a single huge flock that flies high above the Gulf of Mexico. It is thought that this is the way females and males of the species meet to breed. After a short time, the dragons disperse back to their lairs.

Draco americanus tex, right, is known as the moth dragon. This nocturnal, furry, North American plains dragon is thought to be similar to the Amphithere in that it also has no obvious legs.

MOTH DRAGON

Draco americanus tex

The moth dragon hunts buffalo at night, panicking the herds and driving them over convenient nearby cliffs. It is often drawn to the light of camp fires. LAIR—Nestled among giant boulders or rocks. SIZE—15 feet long; 8 to 10 feet high. COLORATION—A rainbow of colours. FORMS OF ATTACK—Frightens its prey. FOOD—Buffalo, mustangs and other large plains dwellers.

Draco americanus incognito, below, is better at concealing its true identity than any other dragon. It dwells in the dense heart of the Amazon jungle and very little is known about either its appearance or habits.

Homework: Write a description of what Draco americanus incognito may be like.

59

LESSON XVII.
A DRAGON-KEEPER'S GUIDE.

As an advanced student, you may apply to the S.A.S.D. for an orphan dragon's egg. The raising of your own dragon chick will assist you greatly in your study of these creatures and you should continue to monitor the dragon after you release it.

Keep eggs on a nest of live coals—kept burning for 36 months. When you see an egg begin to move, give it a bash with a sledgehammer to help the chick hatch.

Day 23

Little Torcher (as I call him) is now becoming a bit of a handful. The pebbles and stones I had carefully covered in shiny paper to suggest treasure are not fooling him any more. Doubtless in pursuit of real gems, he happened upon a flint and proceeded to incinerate the 'den' I had made for him in a corner of my workshop. I very much fear there will be more trouble ahead, even though I have taken the flint away. Indeed, if he were to become angry with me I would ___ become worried about all my workshop equipme___ When such a chick discovers his fire powe___ afraid he may start to set fire to all sor___ things, even my records! Doesn't he re___ have his best interests at heart?

One very important thing to remember is to keep a Personal Record Book. Not only useful in the field, it will prove an essential companion for anyone trying to raise baby dragons. See a page from my own record book, left.

To keep your chicks healthy and happy sacrifices may need to be made—even at Sunday lunchtime.

Dear Dr. Drake,

I feel that I should be given an orphan dragon's egg because...

Yours sincerely,

It is necessary to apply for an orphan dragon's egg by writing a letter to the Secret and Ancient Society of Dragonologists. Keep your request simple and to the point, explaining just what contribution you expect to make to dragon science.

IN order to raise a baby dragon, you must first create a plan for looking after it:

i. Where you will keep it. Some sort of fireproof construction is essential.
ii. How you will feed it. How you will clean it [dragons do not like baths].
iii. How you will train it. How you will use it [not to chase school bullies].
iv. How you will deal with mischievous behaviour [gently].
v. Where, when and how you will release it [not into your neighbour's garden].

Until you have the answers to these questions, you will not be able to begin this work. If any are lacking (the financial resources to feed it, a place to keep it etc.) you must work at getting these in place first. If this means you need to work at your other studies to find an occupation which pays for your dragonology, so be it!

Homework: Create a plan for looking after your baby dragon. Then obtain an egg.

LESSON XVII continued.
DRAGON FIRST AID.

Like sharks and crocodiles, dragons seem naturally resistant to most kinds of infection. However, dragon chicks can be susceptible to various kinds of throat complaint. This may be because the soft tissues of the throat take some time to harden and develop resistance to the flammable venom used for breathing fire. Accidentally swallowed, the venom can have a corrosive action on their developing throats which can cause discomfort and swelling if it is not treated promptly.

There is a no more heart-rending sight for a dragonologist than seeing their charges looking all sad and poorly. Torcher was prone to throat ailments, the onset of which were indicated by a general drooping of wing and horn.

Poor little Torcher was soon getting up to mischief once more—after a dose of my specially formulated linctus. However, it is sometimes easier said than done to get the linctus inside the dragon concerned...

"Ahh! At Last I Can Breathe Fire Again!"

Price: 3s 6d.

WITH
DR. DRAKE'S DRAGON LINCTUS
A SOVEREIGN REMEDY FOR SORE & INFLAMED THROATS.

TIPS ON DRAGON DISEASE DIAGNOSIS.

DRAGON INJURIES.

DRAGONS are prone to the odd injury, mostly caused either accidentally or through fighting with other dragons or a [lucky] dragon slayer. The signs are:

* BLEEDING [avoid contact with fresh dragon's blood or it is you who will become the casualty!]
* HOBBLING
* INABILITY TO FLY
* MAKES SAD 'CHIRPING' NOISES
* TEARS OR GASHES ON THE SKIN
* LOOSE SCALES

Treatment is simple, as dragons have an amazing ability to heal themselves in a very short time and it is rare to see a dragon with scars. Essentially, the dragon must be kept as warm as possible [at least 130 degrees], and be left in peace to recover.

DRAGON ILLNESSES.

DRAGON chicks are only really prone to sore throats, and these are not really illnesses as such, but are a form of internal injury. The signs are:

* DULL EYES [the dragon may well not maintain eye-contact with you]
* DROOPING WINGS
* A 'POORLY' POSTURE
* INABILITY TO FLY
* MAKES 'RASPING' NOISES
* BAD-TEMPERED BEHAVIOUR
* MOUTH CLAMPED SHUT

Treatment here consists of always having a good supply of Dr. Drake's Dragon Linctus. The only problem comes in administering the linctus, for which purpose it may be handy to purchase a very large crowbar, to help in opening the dragon's mouth.

AN EMERGENCY RECIPE FOR DRAGON LINCTUS.

[should supplies of my own patented linctus become unaccountably unavailable].
Mix 12 pints of honey with the juice of 36 lemons and 12 pints of hot water. Add a sprinkling of dragon dust. Administer orally to dragons only [it is dangerous for humans to ingest dragon dust in any quantity], giving 2 pints every 15 minutes, until symptoms subside.

NOTE: There are a number of rare maladies that can afflict dragons. These are most usually caught as the result of a charm or spell going wrong. Treatment of these is its own special study for Dragonological Veterinarians.

Homework: Learn to read the signs associated with a sick dragon. That way, you will be prepared to offer the proper assistance should the time come.

LESSON XVIII.
HOW TO DRAW DRAGONS.

This topic is dealt with as part of Advanced Dragonology because clearly, in order to learn how to draw dragons accurately—a vital skill for any Natural Historian, it is necessary to be able to get close enough to them in the wild. It is also important to remember that speed is of the essence when drawing dragons—as they do not generally make the best 'sitters'.

Try not to get side-tracked when drawing dragons...

A sleeping dragon makes for a nice 'still life' drawing—as long as he or she doesn't wake up.

A dragon in flight makes an interesting, if challenging, object of study.

Note wing shape...

Detail of head...

It takes courage and determination
to get this close to a dragon.

Some dragons can be rather vain—only show them
your efforts if you are sure of a good reception.

*Homework: Begin to practise by sketching some of the illustrations in
this book, then go out and find your own dragons to draw.*

LESSON XIX.
INVENTING DRAGON SCRIPTS.

While it can be very useful to be able to write in ordinary runic dragon script, there are plenty of times when it may be necessary to conceal the content of your messages, even from other dragonologists. In these cases it may be a good idea to invent your own form of script—there is little doubt that a friendly, literate dragon will have no problem picking it up. Additionally, the dragon will probably see learning to use your new script as an interesting challenge, making communication interesting and therefore more likely. Of course, it can also be useful to practise new scripts on your fellow dragonology students. Below are examples of two dragon scripts—one based on Ancient Egyptian hieroglyphs, the other newly invented.

This script is based on the Ancient Egyptian 'alphabet'. It may need to be adapted for everyday use, as some vowel sounds are not represented.

Lambert Script is based on the English Alphabet, but so loosely that it is hard to read. It was invented by the noted dragonologist J. Lambert of Reigate

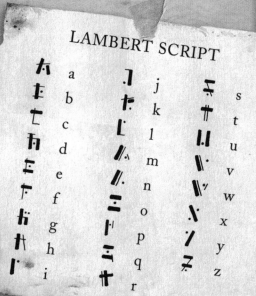

THE EGYPTIAN ALPHABET

	a		i		q	
	a		j		r	
	b		kh		sh	
	d		kh		s	
	f		k		tj	
	g		m		t	
	h		n		w/u	
	h		p		y	

LAMBERT SCRIPT

	a		j		s	
	b		k		t	
	c		l		u	
	d		m		v	
	e		n		w	
	f		o		x	
	g		p		y	
	h		q		z	
	i		r			

_____ SCRIPT

__ a		__ j		__ s	
__ b		__ k		__ t	
__ c		__ l		__ u	
__ d		__ m		__ v	
__ e		__ n		__ w	
__ f		__ o		__ x	
__ g		__ p		__ y	
__ h		__ q		__ z	
__ i		__ r			

WHEN writing your script you may want to make it more complicated than simply having one symbol for 'a', another symbol for 'b' etc. It is possible to achieve this by using special symbols for whole words. In general these should be words that are going to crop up again and again in your dialogue with dragons, such as 'dinner', 'not' and 'me'. Here are some examples from an extended form of Lambert Script:

dinner   *not*   *me*

Homework:

LESSON XX.
DRAGON MAGIC—WORDS OF POWER.

The words on this page are supposedly so powerful that it has been necessary to hide them from those who might be at risk from using them, by resorting to mirror-writing. Hold them up to a mirror, and their secrets will be revealed. All except for the last one are performed in exactly the same way. Each word should be pronounced individually under a blue moon, and the dragonologist merely needs to have a part of the dragon to be commanded about his person, such as a piece of sloughed-off skin.

LYCOTHRAX

belsifer

PYRAMIDE

RIDANTOR

The usages of these four words of dragon power are [in order]—to temporarily alter the form of the dragon into the shape of a cat; to cause the dragon to become temporarily stunned; to make the dragon unaccountably pile up all his treasure; to make the dragon take you from one place to another on his back. Of course, none of these spells should ever be used.

FRANCIS BACON'S MYSTERY REVEALED.

To perform this spell, you must somehow trick the dragon into saying the following word:

HONORIFICABILITUDINITATIBUS

Should you achieve this you may ask the dragon to explain anything to you that lies within his circle of knowledge, and he will do it.

DR. DEE'S MANIFESTATION OF MIRRORS.

This spell simply relies on the magician reading out the words. However, the difficult part is that there must be an arrangement of mirrors, so that both parts can be seen the correct way round at the same time before it is read:

When in the mirror something's seen that never should be spied,
Orthrax will come and tell a doom which cannot be denied,
He'll roar and rage, he'll rage and roar, send out a jet of flame,
And cry, "Fi! Fi! Who Dare Deny, that Orthrax is my name!"

Orthrax, Orthrax, Be calm, I say, wheresoever you may fly,
Out on the dale or in the vale or somewhere way up high,
Oh, come to me and hum to me, lay down your horny head,
and whisper in the fading light where lies your treasure bed.

THE HONG WEI DRAGON TRANSFORMATION.

An immensely powerful spell, the Hong Wei Dragon Transformation has the power to alter the shape of the caster so that they appear to be a medium-sized *lung* dragon of great age and wisdom. To cast it, take five ounces of dragon dust, mixed with basilisk blood, and repeat the words as a mantra:

勿憎恨蛇無角
Wu zeng hen she wu jiao

The spell lasts for three whole days. The translation of the spell is roughly: "Do not despise the snake for having no horns..." and it is the beginning of a well-known phrase that ends, "For who knows, one day he may become a dragon!" The spell is found towards the middle of the second section of the remarkable Dragon Sutra of Hong Wei.

Homework: Commit the contents of this page to memory, then seal it up forever, or destroy it. Do not allow it to fall into the wrong hands!

69

LESSON XXI.
BEGIN YOUR OWN LEGEND.

Equipped with all the most modern dragon-tracking paraphernalia, and with a head full of knowledge, understanding, and compassion, the advanced dragonologist is ready to set out on a lifetime of adventure.

To the student who has completed my course.

My Dear Fellow Dragonologist,

NOW that you have reached an advanced level, there is surely no need for me to reiterate the dangers that may beset the determined dragonologist in his quest to conserve and protect those dragons that still remain, yet perhaps it will not hurt to mention them one last time—the scorn of fools who do not believe in fairies and elves, let alone dragons; the unscrupulous practices of those dragonologists who care more for gold and ill-gotten gains than knowledge and science; and the disruptive ways of those who would exploit every corner of this world of ours merely for gain, caring little for those creatures that stand in their way. All these must be dealt with, and dealt with courageously.

Yet I am confident that, having indeed reached such a deep understanding of dragons as you now have, you will now in no way use it unwisely. I am sure that you will come across other dragonologists during the course of your studies—they are relatively easy to identify, not only because of the specialised kit they carry, but also because of their general love of learning of all kinds. You may like to form a society of dragonologists of your own and, if you do, then you will have access to much greater resources as you pursue your studies.

The main thing to remember is that, if you work hard enough and long enough you will begin to live not only your very own dragon legend but you will help to take dragon science one step further down the road to universal acceptibility, and there can be no greater reward than this.

Yours in Dragonology,

Ernest Drake

CONCLUSION.
FORMING A DRAGONOLOGICAL SOCIETY.

There comes a time when a dragonologist, having completed some such course as this one, will seek out the company of other dragonologists and form a Dragonological Society, where knowledge can be shared and expeditions and experiments jointly undertaken. Any such Society needs a Constitution and so it is suggested that if you wish to form one, you copy the *Declaration of Aims of a Modern Dragonological Society*, created by the founders of the American Dragonological Society who broke away from the S.A.S.D. in 1774, adding a date and name for your Society and asking members who would like to join to sign it. Note: There is no Constitution for the Secret and Ancient Society of Dragonologists, instead it is goverened by the precedents of Dragon Common Law.

THE DECLARATION OF AIMS
OF A MODERN
DRAGONOLOGICAL SOCIETY.

When in the Course of Dragonological events, it becomes necessary for hitherto independent Dragonologists to unite themselves and become connected the one to another as members of a Dragonological Society, and thereby to assume among the Societies of the Earth a certain responsibility to Nature as it exists in Dragon kind, a decent respect to the opinions of mankind requires that they should declare the Laws by which their new formed Society will operate.

We hold these truths to be self-evident, that all Dragons who exist are under a terrible threat of extinction, given mankind's extraordinary capacity for continued expansion across the globe, but that Dragons, like all sentient creatures, ought to be allowed certain inalienable rights to Life, Liberty and the pursuit of Treasure. That to secure these rights Dragonological Societies are instituted among men, deriving from their belief in and experience of Dragons, to study, conserve and protect those dragons that still remain, and to remain secret, subtle and at all times silent about this essential work with those who do not believe, or else claim not to believe, in Dragons. That whenever any Dragonological Society becomes destructive of these ends, it is the right of its members to alter or abolish it, and to institute a new Society, laying its foundation on such sound Dragonological principles, and organising its powers in such form, as to them shall seem most likely to effect the Work of a Dragonologist and promote the honorable science of Dragonology.

We therefore, the Representatives of This Dragonological Society, do solemnly publish and declare by our signatures on the back of this Declaration that we have formed from this ___ day of _____, 19___ a Dragonological Society that shall hereafter be called the _____Society of Dragonologists.

GLOSSARY
OF DRAGONOLOGICAL TERMS.

AMPHITHERE — A very large, feathered, serpentine dragon found mainly in North, Central and South America.

AMULET — A piece of jewellery worn for its magical protective properties; a sort of Charm.

AVELOCA — The dragon of Guadalajara. Dr. Drake first encountered him in a trip to Mexico in 1872. His name means crazy bird.

BASILISK — A dragon of bluebell woods and chalk downland, which is falsely supposed to kill merely by looking at its victims.

BEOWULF — A dragon slayer and hero of a famous Old English poem who encounters Grendel, Grendel's Mother and, finally, a dragon.

COCKATRICE — A creature that is often supposed to be related to dragons, and is confused with basilisks. In fact, its evolution is different.

DRAGON — The large, scaly, usually winged and fire-breathing creature that is the object of study of a dragonologist.

DRAGON DECOY — A sort of dragon costume meant to fool dragons who are being spied on. It should be made from fire-proof material.

DRAGON DUST — A substance that is breathed out by nesting mother dragons, and condenses from their breath—it has numerous uses.

DRAGON LINCTUS — A preparation for the cure of dragons invented by Dr. Drake. Its ingredients are secret, although it contains honey and lemon.

DRAGON MASTER — A person who, by reason of their sure mastery of all things dragonological, is best placed to conserve and protect dragons.

DRAGONOLOGIST	A person who, through the medium of science or legend, studies that noble creature known as a dragon.
DRAGONOLOGY	The study of dragons. In order to be complete, this must involve not only the study of wild dragons, but also of dragon legend.
DRAGON SCRIPT	Most often used to refer to the ancient runes that were allegedly gifted to mankind by the dragons themselves.
DRAGON'S EYE	A particularly powerful magical gem that has the ability to reflect back a budding Dragon Master with perfect clarity.
DRAGON TRAP	The name for a natural rock formation traditionally used to hunt dragons. A sort of natural 'lobster pot'.
DR. ERNEST DRAKE	A gentlemen from St. Leonard's Forest in England, who has made it his business to spread the true knowledge of dragons.
EUROPEAN DRAGON	The classical fire-breathing Western dragon, with wings, scales, an arrowhead tail, claws and horns.
FOOD CHAIN	The most obvious way in which a group of creatures who live in a particular habitat are related.
FROST DRAGON	A northern form of the Western dragon, which has adapted to its polar homelands by being nocturnal and pale in colour.
FU HSI	The legendary Chinese Emperor who was gifted the secret of writing by the Yellow Dragon from the Yellow River.
FUTHARK RUNE [also: FUTHORC]	A runic language said to have evolved in Germanic and Norse countries from Ancient Greek script, actually gifted by dragons.

GARGOUILLE — A French dragon that disguises itself by looking very like a gargoyle. Sometimes said to have an extremely long neck.

KNUCKER — A small Western dragon that lives in underground holes or deep wells, and cannot actually fly.

KNUCKER HOLE — A general name for the lair of any knucker; specifically a place near Lyminster, England, known as the "Knucker Hole".

LAMBTON WORM — A dragon that appears in a legend from the north of England. Set during the crusades, it appears this beast was a knucker.

LUNG — The name, derived from Chinese, given to an Eastern Dragon, particularly the larger and more common sort.

LUNG WEI — One of the dragons of Hong Wei monastery, high in the mountains of south-east China.

LINDWORM — Sometimes used simply to mean dragon; specifically it refers to a particular two-legged, wingless Asian dragon.

MASTER RIDDLER — One who is adept in the decipherment and construction of riddles, and who has survived numerous riddle challenges.

MARSUPIAL DRAGON — The most common type of Australian dragon that rears its young in a fiery pouch and breathes blue smoke.

MERLIN — The founding-father of Western dragonology, Merlin, or Emrys, was also a magician of some passing note.

OLD HOPPY — Perhaps the last marsupial dragon to remain in the Red Centre of Australia, rather than moving to the Blue Mountains.

PETITES-DENTS   A friendly French gargouille and *confidant* of Dr. Ernest Drake, this dragon dwelt on the Isle de la Cité in Paris.

SALAZAAR   A wyvern who was unusually friendly with the tribesmen of the Rif Mountains, known for his habit of slithering about.

TALISMAN   A small stone or other object, often inscribed with mysterious symbols or letters and kept for protective purposes.

THORFAX   An English European dragon who was extensively studied by Dr. Ernest Drake in his youth.

WYVERN   The largest of all dragon species, the wyvern is a two-legged dragon that primarily lives in Africa and Arabia.

PUBLISHER'S NOTE: It is interesting that the original volume of Dr. Drake's course on *Working With Dragons* included a set of gummed stickers. This is highly unusual in the world of Victorian schoolbooks, which tended to view learning as an affair to be taken very seriously, without much in the way of jokes, humour or amusement. Clearly, Dr. Drake saw his aim as being to entertain as well as to educate and so we have reproduced his stickers here, although not in their gummed original form [which would have made for a lot of licking]. We hope that they will provide the student who is doing the course with a source of amusement, and also note that some of them may be useful in the construction of the *Abramelin's Dragon Attractor* talisman.

Dugald A. Steer, Editor, 2004

DRAGONOLOGICAL LABORATORY

DR. DRAKE NEEDS

YOU

HELP CONSERVE & PROTECT WILD DRAGONS NOW!

THE SECRET AND ANCIENT SOCIETY OF DRAGONOLOGISTS

VIM PROMOVET
DRACONIS

The Secret and Ancient Society of Dragonologists
is Proud to Present a

━━━━━◦◦◦◦◦━━━━━

CERTIFICATE OF
DRAGONOLOGICAL ACHIEVEMENT

awarded to

....

━━━━━◦◦◦◦◦━━━━━

Upon his/her Successful Completion of
Dr. Ernest Drake's
Working With Dragons
A Course in Dragonology.

Ernest Drake

*To Whom It May Concern: The Bearer of This Certificate Has Been Specially Licensed
to Direct the Conservation & Protection of Dragons Wheresoever They May Be Found.
Authorised by the S.A.S.D., Wyvern Way, London, England.*